Habitual
Erik Sternberger

Erik Sternberger

Habitual

©2012 Erik Sternberger

Storm	5
Back To You	7
I'd Die For You (Emotions Set In Fire)	9
Dancing With Angels	11
Myself	13
Trash	15
If	17
I Have To Go	19
It Will Always Be You	21
My Traveling Friend	23
I Lost My Favorite Girl	25
Going It Alone	27
Going To…	29
Ships	31
I Found You	33
Passion	35
Still Me	37
Married Years	39
Turn	41
Thank You	43
If You Want Me To	45
Foolish Game	47
A Different Kind Of Love	49
Hands	51
There Will Always Be A Flutter	53
This Is Happiness	55
A Different Path	57
Let's Go Dancing	59
She Cries Alone	61
Bad Day	63
When I'm Ready	65
Going Too Far	67
20 Years	69

Habitual

Storm

I can feel it
And it seems like the end of times
I can sense it
And feel the fire burn inside.

What can I do?
What can I say?
I am torn from you
I have lost my way.

And I will stumble
Never finding
My way through the rumble
Toward healing.

The world is over
And I fall to my knees
As I wait for an end to forever
As I wait for someone to rescue me.

Will there be peace?
Will there be a light at the end?
Will the pain ever cease?
What will happen to my life-long friend?

Waves of devastation
Waves of sorrow
No hope of restoration
Will there be a tomorrow?

Habitual

Back To You

I wake in the morning
With nothing to do
The day is just beginning
And I want to call you.

But it is too early
Should I just go to sleep?
Should I dream of you holding me?
Should I dream of the dreams you keep?

But the day is just beginning
I just have to muddle my way through
I have to suppress the yearning
Until I find my way… back to you.

Habitual

I'd Die For You (Emotions Set In Fire)

I'd die for you
Just lay the cards on the table
And sacrifice it all for you
Because I am ready, willing, and able.

When I first saw you
I knew in a flash
I knew what I had to do
And it didn't affect me much.

In a moment
A change, a conscious desire
An emotion so important
An emotion set in fire.

I'd die for you
Because you are my desire
I'd die for you
My emotions are set in fire.

Habitual

Dancing With Angels

Oh how I miss her
She used to dance so well
We would dance together
And it was like dancing with an angel.

I keep a picture of her
By my bedside
We will always be together
She will always have a place inside.

And I will always think of her
Whenever I hear the sweet music play
I would imagine how we would dance together
Each step, each sway.

And how her dress would move
Comfort her skin so fine
With nothing to prove
The dance will always be mine.

But now she's in God's company
And I am standing still
I will always have memories
And she will forever be dancing with angels.

Habitual

Myself

I can't give you
Miles upon miles of jewelry
I can't buy you
Any house that you see.

I can't open the door
To wonders that astound you
I can't give you any more
Than what I am, what I do.

I wear my heart on my sleeve
And offer myself to you
In hopes that you never leave
In hopes that I please you.

And all that I can offer
Is what I give willingly
All I can offer
Is that best part of me.

Habitual

Trash

What I gave to you
You took for granted
The love I offered you
Was weakly planted.

And now I am left with
Nothing to show
Not even a kiss
To light the road.

Crumpled like paper
Our love is trashed
Nothing lasts forever
Our love has crashed.

Habitual

If

If I could heal your wounds with a kiss
I'd ready my lips
If I could erase your pains with a sweet caress
I'd strengthen my fingertips.

And if I could shoulder your burden
I'd deal with the ache
I'll stay until the pressure is gone
If that is what it would take.

I'll take the pain from you
I'll stand ready and willing
I'll be ready to sacrifice for you
If only to see you smiling.

And when you need me
You should know that I'll be there
I'll take the cuts, I'll bleed
Because I truly do care.

Habitual

I Have To Go

      I am here working
      My eight-hour shift
      Seeing you smiling
      Giving me a lift.

      A phone at my side
      It rings, I answer
      A concerned feeling inside
      Fills me with thunder.

      My day is not for me anymore
      There is only one thing I now know
      I drop everything and rush out the door
      I tell my boss… "I have to go."

Habitual

It Will Always Be You

When I saw you
Looking at me that way
I had nothing important to do
Nothing more to say.

Everything flew out the window
The moment you flowed into my vision
I had no need for sorrow
The misery I felt was gone.

And there was no reason to cry
No need for tears
And I looked back and wondered why
I had wasted so many years.

It was you, my dear
It was always you
The woman I hold dear
The one I will always turn to.

Habitual

My Traveling Friend

If I go that way
Will you follow?
What will you say
To fill the shadow?

I don't want to walk alone
I'd rather take you with me
But if I yearn to find my way home
Will you go home with me?

I have wandered near and far
In search of a memory for two
I have followed a made-up star
And dreamed of something new.

So, will you follow?
Will you stay behind?
Come on, I need a shadow
I need someone to share my mind.

Come on, follow
Be my companion
Be my shadow
Be my travelling friend.

Habitual

I Lost My Favorite Girl

The news came in the mail today
And I cried
There was nothing I could say
I read a goodbye.

There was a letter
With a pretty little stamp
But it didn't make me feel any better
Because my eyes grew damp.

I eased the door shut
And shut out the world
It was okay but
Now I lost my favorite girl.

Habitual

Going It Alone

I walked away
Not knowing where I should go
I shrugged off the day
With nothing to show.

Hands in pocket
I walked against the wind
With a wish to forget
What I have relived.

There was a memory
I don't want to remember anymore
It is not for me
I want to shut that door.

So I walk away
Not knowing where to go
I walk away
I choose to go it alone.

Habitual

Going To...

I have an urge
To get out and have a good time
I have an urge
To let go of my mind.

I want to seek out
Some fun waiting to be had
I want to chase the bad feelings out
And put fun back in the bag.

Because I get so bored
Being stuck inside
There is so much more
Than four walls and a mind.

There will be no time
No limits I can count
There will just be good times
Because that's what life is all about.

Habitual

Ships

When I was younger
I saw the ships sailing away
Into what seemed like forever
Sailing, sailing away.

And so I waited
For the time to come
When the ships everyone anticipated
Would bring about freedom.

We had no need
For riches and gold
We had no need
Of memories so old.

Will there be stories?
Will there be smiles?
Will there be new memories
That stretch for miles?

And so I wait
Knuckles white on the railing
The sea is blue, the hours grow late
As I wait for ships to come sailing.

Habitual

I Found You

It happened one day
I was walking, you were struggling
I stopped and offered a kind word to say
You listened as you controlled your breathing.

I sat with you
Although you told me to go
And now I will always be with you
This little truth you shall always know.

I will listen with an attentive ear
And you will offer fatherly advice
When I am far I will always be near
About this you'll never have to think twice.

I found you
You found me
I'll be there for you
As you will be there for me.

Habitual

Passion

When you touch me like that
I alight with fire
I get a feeling that
Makes me smile.

And when you kiss me
I see all seven wonders
It sends me on a journey
From here to forever.

And that embrace
Indescribable
Face to face
So comfortable.

I see it now
Why I fell so hard for you
Logic takes a final bow
And emotion comes barreling through.

So… continue
I am willing to endure
Anything coming from you
Passion so pure.

Habitual

Still Me

She had to go
Now I'm happier
She had to go
We could no longer stay together.

Two years of hell
I've put up with enough
Two years of hell
I'm not very tough.

She belittled me
And stepped out quite a lot
She harassed me
And gave much less than what she gone.

I'm happier alone
By comparison
Although she kicked me out of my home
And left me with nothing to lean on.

I've guess I've learned
I guess I've suffered plenty
I guess I've had my lifetime burn
But I came out of the fire… I'm still me.

Habitual

Married Years

I'm living with you
I know you inside and out
I wake up next to you
With you, I have no doubt.

All through my days
I don't struggle with a smile
It just stays and stays
For much longer than a while.

And worries go out the window
Boulders are shrugged off
There is no danger in a passing shadow
Or trouble waiting at the next turn-off.

I can live each day
And enjoy every moment of my life
Because I wake up in exactly the same way
I wake up to the smiling face of my wife.

Habitual

Turn

When I need a crutch
I turn to you
When I think too much
I bear my soul to you.

It is you I turn to
Always and forevermore
It will always be you
A picture of trust I will always adore.

With a kind word or a few
I'll turn my troubles to you
I will always turn to you
Because that is what I'll always do.

Habitual

Thank You

I never realized
How much I need you
I just looked into your eyes
And didn't realize what I had to do.

I had to love you
I had to make you smile
I had to adore you
While walking a painful mile.

I had to fight to hold you
When times got tough
I had to embrace you
When my life became just too much.

You just don't realize
I have to give it all to you
From the ache in my shoulders to the sparkle in my eyes
My whole body is built for you.

I will never repay
What you have given me
With just a glance to make me stay
A moment stretched into eternity.

Thank you
Precious darling
Thank you
For rescuing me.

Habitual

If You Want Me To

I will walk through fire
Just to touch your skin
I will climb ever so higher
If you'd just let me in.

I'd go through hell for you
And shake hands with the devil
Anything you tell me to
I'll smile and say that I will.

In all honesty
I'd race against time
I won't even think about me
Or the status of my mind.

If you tell me to
I'd run to hell and back
Trailing the fire that is my due
I'd run without looking back.

Foolish Game

    Why do I walk that way
When I know there'll be danger?
Why can I think of nothing to say
   When confronted with trouble?

      Why do I deny
     A love so true?
    Why do I let fly
Shrugging shoulders at you?

   It is me, I suppose
    I am to blame
   It is me, I suppose
  All part of the game.

Habitual

A Different Kind Of Love

I will never leave you
Even if you wanted me to
Because I am so attached to you
And everything that you do.

When you wake me up for coffee
And ignore me like you sometimes do
I will just shrug and let it be
Because I am still fond of you.

And when you walk away
And leave me wearing a frown
I just don't know what to say
It is your casual way of bringing me down.

I will always forgive
Honey, it's just your way
Just live and let live
That is what I'll always say.

So, hurt me, baby
I can take it in stride
Because I feel that you still love me, baby
And I can feel warmth deep inside.

Habitual

Hands

And as our hands separated
A light went out of your eyes
A deep sorrow of the casually parted
A spot of rain in the bluest skies.

Will we meet again?
When will we touch?
Will it forever rain?
Or is once one more than too much?

My hand is single
A dry mound of flesh
A door with no portal
A screen with no mesh.

My hand needs your hand
Complete the circuit
Don't you understand?
I ache for it.

Habitual

There Will Always Be A Flutter

When I look at you
Even after all these years
I still don't know what to do
To hide all these tears.

You still make me weak at the knees
And I don't mind
You provide me with all sorts of eternities
By giving me a smile so kind.

And when I wake up next to you
Even though normal feelings fade
I am still so in love with you
And am grateful with what you gave.

This love will never go away
Even if we stay together forever
And I will always honestly say
There will always be a flutter.

Habitual

This Is Happiness

We're on the couch
Side by side
Peace within, peace without
Your hand entwined with mine.

What are we watching?
Do we care?
We are just experiencing
I am here, you are there.

There is no other place I'd rather be
No other company I'd rather be with
I'm with you, you're with me
I have this feeling that just won't quit.

Will this night ever end?
Hand in hand
Your presence will constantly send
Me to a wondrous land.

This is happiness
No more, no less
Just extreme loveliness
And feelings I can barely express.

This is happiness
With you, my dear
Embraced in vividness
Holding you so near.

Habitual

A Different Path

I'm thinking of going one way
You're thinking of another
I fight the urge not to stay
When you talk about forever.

I want to walk away
While you walk in another direction
I have nothing useful to say
When all you are is a distraction.

I walk away
You walk away
I call it a day
You say it could be night anyway.

Differing opinions
No solution
Two paths moving on
But without union.

I walk away
You turn around
I choose someplace else to stay
While keeping my head on level ground.

And with a smile
I bid you goodbye
I walk a different mile
With something else in mind.

Habitual

Let's Go Dancing

Underneath the setting sun
Arm in arm
Hands slowly embrace
Locked in by my charm.

I look into your eyes
You look into mine
I overflow with love
There is no meaning to time.

Dancing in silence
Just you and I
Nothing else matters
Caressing eye to eye.

There is no music
No others all around
Nothing to distract
Nothing to hold us to solid ground.

Just you and I
Dancing the night away
Arm in arm
Matching sway with sway.

Perfect unity
Dancing the night away
Arm in arm
There is nothing more to say.

Habitual

She Cries Alone

All around the playground
Laughter drifts to her ears
But the little girl wears a frown
And battles sadness no one hears.

She sits alone
Away from the taunting
But the words won't leave her alone
Constantly biting, constantly haunting.

Even when the day is done
She cries herself to sleep
She cannot tell anyone
The memories are hers to keep.

And she cries
And they tease
Ignoring the tears in her eyes
Ignoring her silent pleas.

She feels down
These should be her best years
But alone on the playground
She sees nothing but tears.

Will it ever end?
Will the teasing ever stop?
Will she find the one saving friend
Who will help her over the top?

Habitual

Bad Day

All alone on the playground
When will the school day be over?
Tears streaming down her face without a sound
A torturous day lasting forever.

Taunts and ridicules
Follow her down the halls
All those kids acting so cool
As they repeat demeaning calls.

All alone on the swings
No one by her side
Thinking hateful things
To shut out voices from outside.

And when she gets home
No one seems to care
She is once again all alone
Even though her family is there.

Tomorrow is another day
When she will wake up an experience
Those kids and their cruel ways
And hurling words that make no sense.

Will they make her cry today?
Will they make her turn away?
Why do kids have to be so cruel?
Why can't she just survive school?

Habitual

When I'm Ready

I won't
Travel down that road
I won't
Do what I'm told.

Until I feel secure
I'll stand still
When there is nothing else to endure
When I strengthen my will.

Until then
You just have to be patient
Because only I can say when
The information will be sent.

So… smile away
And know that I won't be swayed
I will decide on the day
When the debt will be paid.

Habitual

Going Too Far

Don't bother me
I know what I'm doing
This is my life story
I know what's happening.

Growing up
I knew all along
I wasn't one to give up
Even though I knew the path was wrong.

I hacked at the branches
I hiked over the boulders
I dug through the deepest of trenches
I carried it all on my shoulders.

I have a goal
I will attain the dream
I set my eyes on the gold
And I will go until I run out of steam.

Am I going too far?
I don't think so
Because I only live where pleasures are
And that is where I yearn to go.

Habitual

20 Years

It's been twenty years
Since my best friend passed
And throughout the bitter tears
I made life last.

And now I look back
Did I live for him?
Or did I slip off track
Between now and then?

And the page is turned
Memories never fade
The book may be burned
But there are no scars to the page.

I move on
Is it for him?
I move on
Do I do it in memory of him?

www.ingramcontent.com/pod-product-compliance
Lightning Source LLC
Chambersburg PA
CBHW031423040426
42444CB00005B/685